EDWARD ELGAR

Te Deum and Benedictus
Opus 34

for SATB and Organ or Orchestra

Edited by Bruce Wood

NOVELLO

Published in Great Britain by Novello Publishing Limited
(a division of Music Sales Limited)
14/15 Berners Street, London W1T 3LJ

Exclusive distributors: Hal Leonard Europe Limited,
Newmarket Road Bury St Edmunds, Suffolk, IP33 3YB
Order No. NOV320078
www.chesternovello.com

Preface

Elgar composed his *Te Deum and Benedictus* in 1897 at the request of his friend G.R. Sinclair, organist of Hereford Cathedral, for the opening service of the Three Choirs Festival in September that year. He began work on the vocal score at the end of May, and finished it within three weeks; by late June he had concluded an agreement with Novello for its publication, and during July he corrected the proofs and also orchestrated the work. The autograph vocal score is now lost, but in the process of orchestration Elgar changed a good many details of the accompaniment, some of them merely phrasing, articulation or dynamic markings, but others affecting the notes themselves. In consequence, some passages in the autograph full score (London, British Library, Add. MS 57999) are not accurately represented by the organ part in the published vocal score. This new edition of the latter brings it into agreement with the full score; besides numerous emendations involving only the markings, there are more substantial changes in bars 37-38, 54, 98-99, 144, 162, 173, 194-195, 198-200, 210 and 215-218 of the *Te Deum*, and in bars 22-26, 30-31, 49, 68-69, 88, 90, 101-103 and 105 of the *Benedictus*. The full score and orchestral material available on hire from the publishers have also been corrected from the autograph.

Both the vocal and the orchestral score are full of Elgar's characteristic markings of phrasing, articulation and expression, and of his highly specific directions as to flexibility of pulse, which he carefully distinguished from the main tempo indications. He was aware that some performers, especially singers, found his score markings unduly restrictive. "Would you give yourself the trouble", he once wrote to W.G. McNaught of Novello, "to look over a proof [of some part-songs] with an eye – two eyes – to expression-marks and stage directions? I overdo this sort of thing (necessary in orchestral stuff) as I put down all my feelings as I write and then haven't the heart to take 'em out." For the attentive performer, nonetheless, Elgar's markings are as important as the notes themselves.

I am grateful to the Librarians and authorities of the British Library for their unfailing helpfulness, and for permission to consult materials among their holdings in the preparation of this new edition.

BRUCE WOOD
School of Music
University of Wales, Bangor
Summer 2004

To my friend, George Robertson Sinclair

TE DEUM LAUDAMUS

EDWARD ELGAR, Op. 34, No. 1
Edited by Bruce Wood

* ORGAN

* If performed with orchestral accompaniment the organ part in the full score should be used in place of the above arrangement. If the orchestra is not employed the introduction may be curtailed, if desired, by commencing at **B** .

sonore
add 16' & 32' Sw. coupled

H Animato

mf legato

The ho - ly Church through - out all the

world doth ac-know - ledge Thee;

The ho - ly Church through - out all the

The Fa - ther___ of an in - fi-nite

The Fa - ther___ of an in - fi-nite

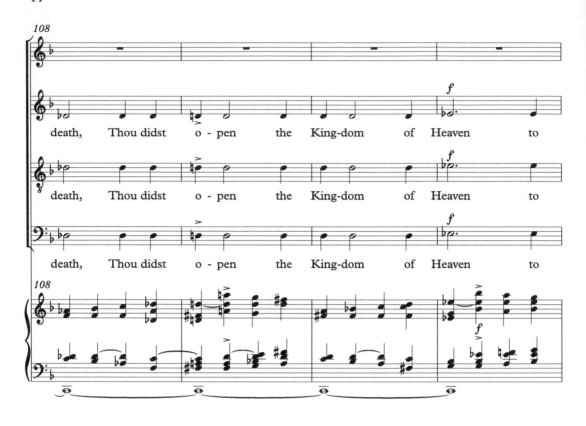

ser-vants, whom Thou hast re - deem-ed with Thy pre - cious blood.

ser-vants, whom Thou hast re - deem-ed with Thy pre - cious blood.

ser-vants, whom Thou hast re - deem-ed with Thy pre - cious blood.

ser-vants, whom Thou hast re - deem-ed with Thy pre - cious blood.

Make— them to be num-ber'd with Thy Saints, in

Make— them to be num-ber'd with Thy Saints, in

Make— them to be num-ber'd with Thy Saints,

Make— them to be num-ber'd with Thy Saints,

BENEDICTUS

EDWARD ELGAR, Op. 34, No. 2
Edited by Bruce Wood

spake by the mouth of His Ho - ly Pro-phets, which have been since the world be -

spake by the mouth of His Ho - ly Pro-phets, which have been since the world be -

spake by the mouth of His Ho - ly Pro-phets, which have been since the world be -

spake by the mouth of His Ho - ly Pro-phets, which have been since the world be -

C *pp* *espress.*

- gan; That we should be sav - ed from our en - e - mies,

- gan;

- gan;

- gan;

C

[Ped.]

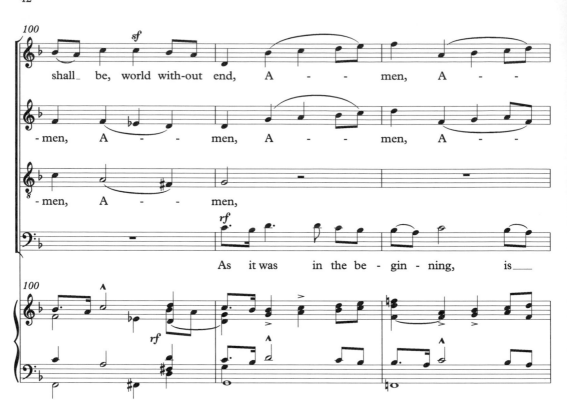